On-the-Job

MATH
MYSTERIES

On-the-Job

MATH
MYSTERIES

REAL-LIFE MATH FROM EXCITING CAREERS

MARYA WASHINGTON TYLER

Routledge
Taylor & Francis Group

NEW YORK AND LONDON

First published in 2009 by Prufrock Press Inc.

Published in 2021 by Routledge
605 Third Avenue, New York, NY 10017
2 Park Square, Milton Park, Abingdon, Oxon OX14 4RN

Routledge is an imprint of the Taylor & Francis Group, an informa business

Copyright © 2009 Taylor & Francis Group

Photos by Kip Micheal Tyler
Production Design by Marjorie Parker

ISBN: 9781593633257 (pbk)

DOI: 10.4324/9781003236924

Dedication

My heartfelt thanks to all the kind folks who contributed
so freely to this book.

Mathematics is singing in the trees,
seeping out of every rock,
whispering when the wind is still.

Contents

About This Book

Did you ever imagine that instead of teaching math within the classroom, you could take your students on field trips across the country to meet with real people who are actively engaged in doing real-life math? All over the world, in every city and town, every single day of the year there are real people facing real problems that require real mathematical solutions. Sometimes the correct solution will save a life (and the opposite is true!) What if you and your students could meet with these people and help them find solutions for their math problems?

Before you is a compendium of those field trips. Between the front and back covers of *On-the-Job Math Mysteries: Real-Life Math From Exciting Careers* you will meet 24 diverse people involved in some of the most intriguing professions in America's Pacific Northwest. Each section will bring you and your students face to face with unique individuals— individuals who will share engaging mathematical challenges. These friendly folks will talk to your students in their own words, sometimes sharing a bit of advice for life, and your students will do their math.

On-the-Job Math Mysteries is geared to high-ability students in grades 4–8, but could be fun for students of higher grades. Each section is best worked on in small groups or with the whole class, but it also could be used by students working individually.

I have had a great deal of success teaching mathematics to gifted students over the past 15 years, and this book is created with an understanding of gifted students, an understanding of mathematics, and a respect for the national standards in mind. You will find the problems in this book parallel the National Council of Teachers of Mathematics (NCTM) standards, first of which is the use of mathematics to solve problems. Likewise, students who are closely involved in the problems they are solving will be more inclined to apply logical reasoning as they design their procedures and justify their solutions. You will find that the NCTM standards, such as selecting an operation, determining place value, using fractions and decimals, working with geometry, applying measurement skills, estimating, and recording and analyzing data, will take on real importance to students while they develop numerical fluency and algebraic thinking solving the real-world problems presented here.

On-the-Job Math Mysteries is as close as you can get to real life between the pages of a two-dimensional text. Working with the engaging and diverse mathematics presented here by colorful people, your students will see exactly what is at stake in problem solving, why mathematics is essential, and why accuracy matters.

Have a wonderful trip!

Note to Students

If you're like me, you like the way math makes your brain feel. It's a rush, a lot like runners' high, but easier to come by. When you examine a mathematics problem, neurons forge new pathways, venturing off into unexplored areas of your brain.

Another thing I like about math is that it's pure. Mathematics is not affected by war or global warming. It doesn't lie. It doesn't whine, or bite, or have fleas. It's reasonable, even when the rest of the world is not.

One more thing. Math is enduring. The principles of mathematics are the same today as they were at the initial "Poof," which set the universe in motion. 7 + 4 was 11 then, and it still is.

—Marya Washington Tyler

Ringmaster
Justin Loomis

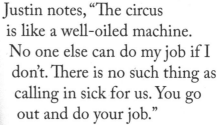

Justin Loomis has been with the circus as long as he can remember. When most kids were going to school and playing baseball, Justin was working as a clown. According to Justin, "If you grow up in the business like I did, you receive very little schooling." Now, Justin highly values education and schooling.

At the age of 15, Justin turned from clowning to announcing, and he has worked for the circus through rain or shine ever since. "I've worked in hurricanes; I've worked in tornados. There have been times when we've come pretty close to seeing the tent fly away."

But, the show must go on! Amazingly, there are no sick days for circus people.

Justin notes, "The circus is like a well-oiled machine. No one else can do my job if I don't. There is no such thing as calling in sick for us. You go out and do your job."

People may question whether math is involved in the circus life. "We use mathematics all day long. For our high wire acts, and for most of our acts, measurements have to be

precise. The cables, the ropes, the pulleys, the stakes—everything has to be exact."

When asked what the best part is of being in the circus, Justin responds, "It's helping people forget about their troubles while they're here. At the end of the day, when everyone walks out with a smile, I feel like I've done my job."

Below is a rough drawing of the Circus Gatti setup as viewed from above. The three show rings are exactly 42 feet in diameter. The distance from pole ✛ to pole ✛ is exactly 47 feet. The guy wires (⟶) that hold up both end poles are staked to the ground 57 feet out, as measured along the ground.

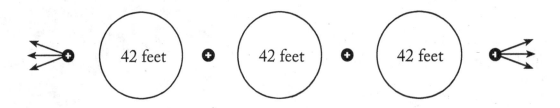

1. How wide does the arena need to be in order to accommodate the Circus Gatti?

Elephant Trainer
John Pelton

CIRCUS GATTI

John Pelton has three coworkers: Tika, Patti, and Wanda. Wanda weighs 7,500 pounds, Patti is about the same size, and Tika weighs 8,500 pounds. Tika and Patti are in their 40s, and Wanda is 55 years old. Wanda, Patti, and Tika are, of course, elephants.

Besides hay, grain, carrots, apples, watermelon, and the occasional peanut butter sandwich, John feeds the elephants vitamin supplements. According to John, "The directions call for 1.25 pounds of vitamins per 100 pounds of body weight." John says the elephants also like Fruit Loops. "Elephants have a sweet tooth, just like we do—only theirs is much bigger."

2. How many pounds of vitamins should John feed Wanda?

3. About how many pounds of vitamins should John feed Patti?

4. How many pounds of vitamins should John feed Tika?

High Wire Acrobat
Cristian Toscano

"We just have to balance and concentrate a lot," says 11-year old Cristian Toscano, who performs with his family in the high wire act, when asked about his role in the circus. Acrobats jump rope, leap, spin, and stand on top of each other's shoulders while all of them are balanced on a skinny wire 25 feet above the ground. Did I mention there is no net to catch them?

Circus performers spend most of their time traveling to new places all around the world. For example, one week, the Toscanos will be in South America and soon after that, they will travel to Saudi Arabia to perform. Because of the constant travel, Cristian almost never goes to school, but studies on the road. Cristian explains, "We get school books through the mail. My favorite subject is math. I like doing math and I like doing high wire . . . both the same."

5. Given that each story of a normal building is approximately 10 feet tall, how many stories high is Cristian's high wire?

Giggling Goat Garden	Organic Farmer

Organic Farmer
Katrinka Hibler

Katrinka has 10 contented cows, 86 squabbling chickens, and 19 giggling goats on 40 acres of bountiful farmland. Does being a farmer require math? Of course! As Katrinka notes, "There's plenty of math in farming. I wish I remembered geometry better than I do."

In fact, Katrinka has a problem to solve that involves math: "Right now I'm trying to figure out how much water I'll need to water my one-acre berry patch. I know an acre is 43,560 square feet, but I don't need 43,560 cubic feet of water. I only want the water an inch deep."

1. How many cubic feet of water does Katrinka need?

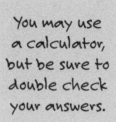

You may use a calculator, but be sure to double check your answers.

2. According to Katrinka, "About 7.5 gallons will fit in one cubic foot." How many gallons of water does she need for her berry patch?

Katrinka grows just about every kind of vegetable you've ever heard of, and a few you probably haven't heard of (purple cauliflower?). Eighteen families subscribe to Katrinka's Community Supported Agriculture (CSA). Subscribing to a CSA is like subscribing to a magazine, but her customers receive homegrown fruits and vegetables instead of magazines.

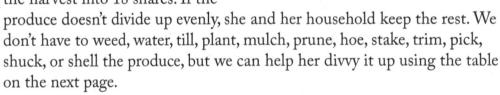

Every week, Katrinka divides the harvest into 18 shares. If the produce doesn't divide up evenly, she and her household keep the rest. We don't have to weed, water, till, plant, mulch, prune, hoe, stake, trim, pick, shuck, or shell the produce, but we can help her divvy it up using the table on the next page.

Name:_____ Date:_____

Total Amount Picked (lb = pound)	Smallest Possible Share	Each Share	Leftovers
57 zucchinis	Figure to the nearest whole zucchini		
100 tomatoes	Figure to the nearest whole tomato		
39 lb of rhubarb	Figure to the nearest lb		
3 gallons of blackberries	Figure to the nearest pint		
5 gallons of peas (5 lb per gallon)	Figure to the nearest lb		
58 dahlias	Figure to the nearest flower		
5 lb of basil	Figure to the nearest ¼ lb bunch		
9 lb of kale	Figure to the nearest ½ lb		
12 lb of beet greens	Figure to the nearest ½ lb		

Dogsled Musher
Ray Redington, Jr.

The Iditarod has been described as the longest, most grueling race over the roughest terrain in the world. Fewer than 100 mushers attempt this race across the vast Alaskan wilderness—and with good reason. Obstacles include the distance, weather, and dangerous conditions, among others.

The Distance

No one knows for sure the actual distance of the Iditarod because the trail winds through incredibly rugged terrain. The best estimates lay close to 1,200 miles long.

1. If a dog team runs 120 miles a day, how many days will it take to finish the race?

The Cold

Mushers like Ray prepare for the extreme cold encountered on the trail. At temperatures 30 below zero, with even moderate winds of 30 miles per hour, human flesh freezes solid in 30 seconds. (That's known as the 30-30-30 rule). On the Iditarod trail, temperatures can dip to 80 below (F).

2. If your room temperature is a comfortable 68 degrees F, how much colder would it be on the Iditarod trail?

© Taylor & Francis Group • *On-the-Job Math Mysteries*

8

DOI: 10.4324/9781003236924-3

The Load

Each team is allowed 16 dogs, usually a mix of Siberian Husky and wolf or Irish setter. One time a racer used a team of poodles! (He didn't win.) A long-distance sled dog eats more than 10,000 calories per day, compared to the 2,500 calories dogs in kennels eat per day.

3. If a kennel dog eats two dishes of dog food a day, how many dishes would she eat while running the Iditarod?

Dog musher talk: "Gee" means right, "Haw" means left

The Difficulties

Dogs can lose all of their body fat and half of their protein and survive, but if they lose even 20% of their water, they will die. Mushers need to be sure their dogs get at least a gallon of water per day.

4. How many cups of melted snow are needed for each dog per day?

5. How many cups are needed for a full team of 16 dogs?

The Weather

Mushers also know to expect white-out conditions, snow so intense and fierce that they can't see their dogs, much less the trail. No navigational aids are allowed in the race, so mushers sometimes spend days lost in the wilderness.

The Danger

Thinking about heading up to Alaska to become a dog musher? Watch out for moose! In 1985, a moose attacked Susan Butcher's team during the race, killing two of her dogs and injuring most of the others. However, Susan bounced back to win the next three Iditarod races.

6. In 1973, the first year of the race, the winner finished in 20 days, 49 minutes. Ray's fastest time so far is 9 days, 21 hours, 26 minutes. How much faster was Ray than the first year's winner?

Name:_____ Date: _____

Beekeepers
Dan and Judy Harvey

Dan Harvey gets stung by a bee at least once a day. According to Dan, "The stinger will keep on pumping venom after the bee has flown, so the quicker you get the stinger out the better. Try to scrape the stinger out in the direction it came from."

Fruits and vegetables rely upon bees for pollination, but recent outbreaks of disease have put the critters in peril. Dan and Judy are beekeepers, but they also are bee scientists, working to raise disease-resistant bees without the use of chemicals. Dan explains, "We have about 50 colonies of bees right now. In an average year, a colony will make 100 pounds of honey, while in a good year, we can get 300 pounds per colony."

1. How much honey can Dan and Judy expect to collect in an average year?

2. "How much more honey will we collect in a good year than in an average year?" questions Dan.

According to Dan, "Once collected, we store it [the honey] in barrels that each hold 640 pounds of honey."

3. How many barrels will Dan and Judy need in order to store an average year's honey? (Round to the nearest whole barrel.)

You may use a calculator, but be sure to double check your answers.

DOI: 10.4324/9781003236924-4

Honey weighs 22 ounces per pint. A gallon of water weighs 8 pounds.

4. How many ounces more does a pint of honey weigh than a pint of water? (Hint: Drawing a picture may help.)

Bees live just 6 weeks. During those 6 weeks of summer, the queen bee will lay 1,000 eggs a day. Other than laying eggs, the queen bee doesn't do anything. She doesn't even feed herself. Feeding the queen is left up to nurse bees, who secrete protein-rich royal jelly. How many nurse bees are needed to keep a queen well-fed? "I've had to figure out these equations on my own. You can't just pick up a book and read about this," says Dan.

Some beekeepers say you need a can the size of a corned beef hash can full of bees in order to provide for one queen. A corned beef hash can will hold about a cup of bees, and a cup of bees weighs ¼ pound.

5. When Dan followed this advice, how many pounds of nurse bees did he provide in order to feed 84 queens?

Dan and Judy enjoy their work. Dan concludes, "The world of bees is a subtle, microscopic world. If you don't learn something new every time you go out in the bee yard, you're not looking."

Kayak Guide
Gillian Edwards

In Australia, where Gillian Edwards grew up, math is called "maths." Gillian deals with all kinds of maths now as an Alaskan kayak guide.

Recently, Gillian described her plan for the day, "Today, I will be taking 5 trips out to paddle around Orcas Cove. On these trips, we always have at least 1 guide along for every 6 guests. All of the guests will paddle in double (2-person) kayaks, unless they have young children. Young children sit in the middle of triple kayaks, between 2 adults. The guides use a single kayak, unless there is space left in a double."

Complete the chart below to show how many guides, how many triple kayaks, how many double kayaks, and how many single kayaks will be needed for each trip described below.

1. Trip #1: Eight adults, two teenagers, two young children

2. Trip #2: Eight adults, one older kid, two young children

3. Trip #3: Four adults, one teenager, two young children

	Guides	Triple Kayaks	Double Kayaks	Single Kayaks
Trip #1				
Trip #2				
Trip #3				

© Taylor & Francis Group • *On-the-Job Math Mysteries*

13   DOI: 10.4324/9781003236924-5

Gillian shares this information, "I'm taking four people out for a 5-day, 4-night trip. For snacks, I bring 2 ½ energy bars per person per day."

4. How many energy bars should Gillian bring?

The group plans to paddle south to Grace Creek, a distance of 5 miles, in time for lunch. The group paddles at 3 miles per hour if there is no current or wind.

5. How long will it take Gillian's group to get to Grace Creek under these conditions?

Gillian tells her kayakers, "There is a current due to the tide. I know the current will be flowing south at 1 mile per hour all morning. Because we're headed south, we can add the current speed to our speed."

6. How long will it take the group to reach Grace Creek with the tide?

"It takes me 45 minutes to strike my tent and prepare breakfast, after which I wake up everyone else. It takes the group 30 minutes to eat breakfast and 60 minutes to strike camp and pack the kayaks," describes Gillian.

7. What time does Gillian have to get up so that the group reaches Grace Creek before the current goes slack at 11:34 a.m.?

Shellfish Farmer
Frank Bishop

Little Skookum
Shellfish Growers

In 1927, 11-year-old Frank Bishop made 28 cents a week peddling newspapers. In 2007, his shellfish business made 2.5 million dollars. For six generations, the Bishop family has been raising shellfish (oysters, clams, and geoducks [pronounced goo-ey-ducks]) in Little Skookum Inlet in Washington State.

Clams bury themselves deeply in the sand, where they filter the sea water as it washes over them. If you see a squirt of water coming from a hole in the sand at low tide, you can bet it's a clam.

1. A large oyster can filter up to 7 gallons of water an hour. A clam will filter about half that amount. How many gallons of water can a clam filter an hour?

Digging for clams isn't as easy as it looks. Trouble is, the clams dig away from you just as fast as you dig toward them.

2. Even so, a good digger like Shane (seen at right) can fill a 5-gallon bucket with clams in just 9 minutes. How many buckets can Shane expect to fill during the 3 hours before the tide comes in?

Shane has worked for Little Skookum Shellfish Growers for a long time, and in those years he's dug a lot of clams. Let's find out how many.

3. Shane explains, "One of those socks you see in the photo contains about 30 pounds of clams. I average 100 socks every 2 weeks." How many pounds of clams does Shane average every 2 weeks?

4. If there are 22 clams in each pound, how many clams does Shane dig every 2 weeks?

5. How many clams is that a year?

6. If Shane has been digging for clams for 13 ½ years, how many clams total has he dug?

Check out a video on geoducks: http://dsc.discovery.com/videos/dirty-jobs-gooey-ducks.html

County Judge
Honorable Judge Meadows

You don't want to come before this woman when she's sitting on the bench. It can only mean one thing—you're in trouble.

Judge Meadows is kind, understanding, and good-humored, but when she's behind the bench she's responsible to see that justice is meted out—and that means people who break the law must pay.

When asked if she uses math in her workday, Judge Meadows replies, "Yes, we deal with numbers every day. Witnesses often bring in mathematics for evidence, such as the financial dealings of the accused, or the coefficient of friction in accident reconstruction cases. I have to be able to recognize errors immediately."

She goes on to say, "The jury determines whether the accused is guilty or innocent, and if guilty, it is the judge's responsibility to impose the sentence. When sentencing, I take into account the possibility of 'good' time, which means that if the accused does not cause trouble in jail, he or she will be released after serving ⅔ of the sentence."

Judge Meadows relates a common occurrence: "A woman was put in jail for a probation violation. By the time she is brought to court, she has already served 20 days while in custody. I am assured that she is ready to be released to a responsible life, so I consider the time she spent in custody as time served."

1. How long of a sentence should Judge Meadows impose, if 20 days was ⅔ of it?

2. If a juvenile male has been in custody for 16 days of a 45-day sentence, and earns good time, how many more days will he remain in jail before being released?

What is it like in jail?
- You can't leave.
- There are three people housed in an 8 x 5 foot room.
- You get fresh air maybe once or twice a week.
- The only activity is playing cards or watching TV.
- There is very little or no freedom.

According to Judge Meadows, "A typical DUI (Driving Under the Influence of Alcohol or other Drugs) has a mandatory minimum sentence, which includes 45 days in jail and 90 days wearing an electronic monitoring bracelet. The maximum sentence, which includes both jail time and the electronic monitoring, is 365 days."

3. If a person convicted of a DUI completes the minimum sentence and then is released, how many days did he or she serve?

4. How many days less than the maximum sentence did that person serve?

"The logic involved in solving math problems transcends math. It carries over into all of life," notes Judge Meadows. "Being a judge isn't easy. I deal with criminals every day. However, the rewards are seeing people change their lives for the better."

Railroad Engineer
Dave Buben

Engineers use plenty of math—and Dave does most of it in his head. According to Dave, "We have to keep track of how many cars are on each track, or they might smash into each other."

Dave describes a common problem: "Our train takes logs from the sort yard to the mill, which is about 10 miles away. A string of 26 rail cars waiting to be loaded would be so long it would block the street, so we have to split the train in half and do half at a time."

1. What's half of 26?

2. What's half of 34?

3. What's half of 47?

> Engineers can't see the ends of our cars. That's why it's so important not to trespass on railroad property.

"Once we're loaded, we put the string of cars back together. We might have 26 log cars, then add 7 more log cars, and then add 12 cars full of green lumber."

4. Now how many cars does Dave have?

© Taylor & Francis Group • *On-the-Job Math Mysteries*
19
DOI: 10.4324/9781003236924-8

In describing a typical day at work, Dave shares, "At 7:00 a.m. we load the train with logs, which might take 1 or 1 ½ hours. Then we head for the mill. It's only about 10 miles away, but we've got some pretty good hills between here and there. The train generally goes 10 to 15 miles per hour. If it's raining, or there are wet leaves on the track, we might lose traction. In that case, we 'double the hills,' which means we have to leave 7 or 8 cars off to the side while the train crawls up the hill, and then we have to go back and get them. This could take another ½ hour.

"At the mill, we swap the string of cars we brought for cars needing to go back to the log yard. This procedure takes about 20 minutes. If we're carrying empty cars, the trip back takes only about 20 minutes. If the cars are full, we have to take it easy coming down the hills, so the trip takes about 70 minutes."

5. Given the information Dave shared, what is the least amount of time one round trip might take, including loading time?

6. What is the longest amount of time they would expect it to take?

"Study your math; learn the formulas. Practice the ones that are hard for you. Learn them, and you'll never forget."

Name: _____ Date: _____

Of course, railroad math gets a bit more complicated than this. Check out the formula for designing railroad track below:

$$\tan \tfrac{1}{2}O = \frac{gn}{R_m}$$

$$R_t = \frac{gn}{\tan \tfrac{1}{2}(O - F)}$$

$$E = 2(R_m + \tfrac{g}{2})\sin \tfrac{1}{2}O$$

Videographer
Kip Micheal Tyler

Ever find yourself between a mother bear and her cub? Ever have a killer whale swim under your kayak? Ever been face-to-face with a pack of wolves? It's all in a days work for wildlife videographer Kip Micheal Tyler.

> "The joy of videography for me is the intense realization of the beauty of nature—being able to experience it, record it, and share it without really disturbing it."

Bear Country Video

He shares information about his upcoming adventure: "I'm headed out on a 5-day climbing trip in the Bighorns of Wyoming, and I want to carry as little weight as possible. In addition to 15.5 kilograms of food, water, and other gear, I need to bring quite a load of camera equipment." His items are listed below.

Video camera . . . . 896 grams
Tripod. . . . . 2.8 kilograms
Telephoto lens . . . . 112 grams
Wide angle lens . . . . 84 grams
5 batteries . . . . 126 grams each
Solar charger. . . . . 196 grams
10 mini-DV tapes. . . . . . 28 grams each
Microphone . . . . 56 grams
Camera bag. . . . . 98 grams

1. With the 15.5 kg of food and camp gear, how many kilograms (to the nearest tenth) will he be carrying when the camera gear is added?

"The solar charger allows me to carry only 5 batteries. Without the charger, I would have needed to take 17 batteries."

2. How much weight will he save by taking the solar charger?

Video clips are measured in hours : minutes : seconds : frames. There are 60 minutes in an hour and 60 seconds in a minute; the camera takes 30 frames in a second. The three clips K. Micheal plans to use are 00:02:14:12 and 00:01:03:25 and 00:03:42:15. Credits add another 5 seconds.

3. How long is his video?

The flute music he wants to accompany the video is 7 minutes and 18 seconds long.

4. Which is longer, the song or the video, and by how much?

Heavy Equipment Operator
Patsy Finney

Patsy Finney belongs to the Brown Bear clan of the Tongass tribe of the Tlingit Nation. Tlingit people have lived in Southeast Alaska since the huge glaciers melted away about 10,000 years ago. Patsy is a heavy equipment operator. Right now her job is driving a dump truck on Gravina Island, where she is helping to construct the new airport runway.

Patsy shares, "There are six dump-truck drivers working on this project. It takes each of us 10 minutes to pick up a truckload of rock at the rock pit, deliver it to the runway site, and return."

1. "How many dump-truck loads will I be able to deliver in an hour?"

The workers work from 8:00 a.m. to 4:00 p.m. with no breaks for lunch.

2. How many dump-truck loads will Patsy be able to deliver in a day?

Patsy reflects, "Actually, we do get a chance to stretch twice a day while we wait for airplanes to take off or land nearby. Each wait is 20 minutes long.

3. Factoring in the stretch breaks, how many dump-truck loads can Patsy actually deliver in a day?

4. How many dump-truck loads can the six drivers deliver in a day?

DOI: 10.4324/9781003236924-10

Sometimes the front-end loader at the rock pit has to be fueled up, and one of the dump-truck drivers will have to wait. This means an additional break of about 10 minutes a day for two of us.

5. Given this information, how many total dump-truck loads can the six drivers deliver each day?

Each of Patsy's dump trucks carries 15 yards of rock. A "yard" is really a cubic yard, which means it is one yard long by one yard wide by one yard deep.

6. How many cubic feet are there in a "yard"? (Hint: The answer is not 3.)

7. If each yard of rock weighs ¾ of a ton, how much does a full dump-truck load of rock weigh? Find to the nearest ¼ ton.

8. How many tons of rock does Patsy haul in one good day? Use the answer to question 3, and find to the nearest half ton.

According to Patsy, "Really, it's a little more complicated. As the runway gets longer, we have to take each load a little farther. That means that each load takes a little longer than the one before."

Hey, check this out! For more information on hydraulic machines, visit http://science.howstuffworks.com/hydraulic.htm.

Wildlife Veterinary Tech
Tim Lebling

Tim Lebling has what might be the best job in the world—taking care of sick, wounded, and orphaned sea animals. His job is especially important because there has been a widespread decline of harbor seals, sea lions, and other marine birds and mammals in the Gulf of Alaska. The numbers of Pacific harbor seals counted near Aialik Glacier has decreased from more than 1,600 seals in 1980 to current counts of about 200 seals. The population of Steller sea lions has declined by about 80%. The good news is that devoted scientists and researchers like Tim Lebling are working to change all that.

Tim describes his current work situation: "Right now I'm coming in at 11:00 p.m. and staying until noon, taking care of an orphaned baby sea otter pup that requires round-the-clock care."

1. How many hours a day does Tim work?

According to Tim, "Sea otters require 30% of their body weight a day of clams, squid, crab, and mussels."

2. If a sea otter weighs 50 pounds, how many pounds of food does Tim need to feed him each day?

3. If Tim wanted to give him equal parts of each food, how much of each would he give him?

4. A sea otter pup needs to eat every 3 hours around the clock. How many times do they eat every 24 hours?

5. " How much of each food would I give him at each feeding?" (Find answer to nearest quarter pound.)

Tim often has to treat sick or injured animals: "A dose of antibiotics is required for a sick sea lion. The label says the dose is 35mL per each kilogram the animal weighs. The sea lion weighs 22 kg."

6. How many mL does Tim need for the sea lion?

"While listening to the a heart rate of a ringed seal, I count 23 beats every 15 seconds," says Tim.

7. How many beats per minute is the seal's heart rate?

"When the animals are well, we release them into the wild, and track their movement with a satellite tag. A satellite tag is programmed to transmit every 3 days," explains Tim.

8. If the battery lasts for 230 transmissions, how may days will the satellite tag last?

"There's a start—There's lot more math . . . but I've got to get back to work."

Check us out on the Web:
http://www.alaskasealife.org

Microsoft® Software Engineer
David Washington

David Washington began fixing computers for people in elementary school. The summer before fifth grade, he built his own computer. In the summer before sixth grade, he cowrote a math book called *It's Alive!* Now David helps design software and write code for Microsoft Corporation. Every time your computer does what you ask it to do, it's because a software engineer like David wrote the code for it to do so.

David explains, "As people expect more from computers, software becomes increasingly complex. The challenge for software engineers is to handle more complexity without slowing performance. One of the ways we do this is by minimizing the number of times that the computer has to look at each element, which is called 'walking the list.' The fewer times the computer has to 'walk the list' the better.

"For example, what if you had a list of six students and you wanted to put them in order by age? It is easy for your brain to look over the whole list and put the students in order. The computer, however, can only look at one element at a time, and ask a question like, 'Is your age less than this other person's age or not?'

"To sort the ages of six students (Annie, Bud, Cedric, Dan, Edgar, Flossie), a particular computer asks two questions:

Is your age equal to _____'s age?
Is your age less than or equal to _____'s age?"

1. Use the following information that the computer received to arrange the six students by age (youngest to oldest). If any two ages are equal, put them in alphabetical order by name.

A ≤ B? Yes.
A = B? No.
B ≤ C? No.
A ≤ C? Yes.
A = C? No.
B ≤ D? No.
D ≤ E? Yes.
D = E? No.
E ≤ B? Yes.
E = B? No.
E ≤ F? No.
F ≤ D? Yes.
F = D? Yes.

2. There are three possible outcomes. Can you find all three?

According to David, "The trick to computer science is turning complicated problems into simple ones." Here's a common interview question. It looks complicated, but it's really quite simple:

Prime numbers are numbers that can only be divided by themselves and by 1:

2, 3, 5, 7, 11, 13, 17, 19, 23, 29, 31, 37, 41, 43, 47, 53, 59, 61, 67, 71, 73, 79, 83, 89, . . .

Twin primes are prime numbers that differ by 2:
2, <u>3, 5</u>, <u>7</u>, <u>11, 13</u>, <u>17, 19</u>, 23, <u>29, 31</u>, 37, <u>41, 43</u>, 47, 53, <u>59, 61</u>, 67, <u>71, 73</u>, 79, 83, 89, . . .

Between each twin prime is a number (such as 6, 12, and 18) we'll call **in-betweens.**

3. Prove that all in-betweens (with the exception of 4) are divisible by 6.

"If you get this right, look us up in a couple years."

Name:_____ Date: _____

Environmental Health Specialist
Rose Swier

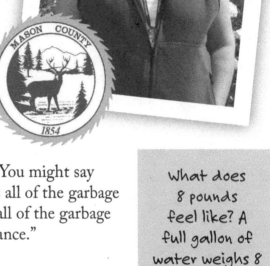

Rose Swier is affectionately called the "garbage police." Her job is to make sure all of the garbage we accumulate is taken care of in a way that won't harm the environment. The problem is . . . there is so much of it.

"Nobody goes to the store to buy garbage," Rose says. "However, on any trip to the store a whole lot of what you bring home is just packaging. Worse yet, most of the packaging is plastic, which comes from oil.

"The average person—man, woman, child, and baby—generates 8 pounds of garbage a day. You might say that you don't make that much, but that includes all of the garbage involved in making everything we use. Think of all of the garbage involved in the process of making paper, for instance."

> What does 8 pounds feel like? A full gallon of water weighs 8 pounds.

1. If you produce 8 pounds of garbage a day, how much do you produce in a week?

Have you ever tried to carry that much weight on your back?

2. How much garbage do you produce in the average month? (30.5 days)

3. How much garbage do you produce in the average 365-day year?

4. How much garbage do you produce in a decade? (Not counting leap years.)

© Taylor & Francis Group • *On-the-Job Math Mysteries*
DOI: 10.4324/9781003236924-13

Rose's job is to inspect facilities that handle solid waste. She explains, "Because tires can catch fire easily, and are breeding grounds for mosquitoes, there is a rule that you are only allowed to have 800 tires lying around. I don't have all day to count tires, but because I know there are about 10 tires in a cubic yard, all I have to do is find the volume. Easy!"

5. A pile of tires is 5 feet tall by 20 feet wide by 27 feet long. What's its volume in cubic feet?

A cubic yard (3 feet × 3 feet × feet) equals 27 cubic feet.

6. How many cubic yards is the pile?

7. Rose questions, "Is the pile in violation?"

Not everyone is pleased that Rose is working so hard to preserve the environment: "I wrote a ticket to a man for dumping a truckload of computer monitors along the side of the road. He told me he knows where I live, and threatened to turn my house into a dump."

In just one year, Americans throw away:

26,800,000 tons of food	2,230,000 tons of newspapers
8,550,000 tons of furniture and furnishings	2,060,000 tons of appliances
6,330,000 tons of clothing and footwear	1,520,000 tons of magazines
5,190,000 tons of glass beer and soda bottles	1,170,000 tons of wine/liquor bottles
4,200,000 tons of plastic wrap and bags	970,000 tons of paper plates and cups
3,650,000 tons of junk mail	840,000 tons of books
3,470,000 tons of diapers	830,000 tons of beer and soda cans
3,160,000 tons of office paper	780,000 tons of towels and sheets
3,070,000 tons of tires	540,000 tons of telephone directories
2,820,000 tons of carpets and rugs	450,000 tons of milk cartons
160,000 tons of lead-acid (car) batteries	

Note. From Hattman, J. (2005, November/December). Talkin' trash: Reduce, reuse, rejoice: Heaps of garbage becomes piles of possibilities. *Sierra.* Retrieved June 12, 2008, from http://www.sierraclub.org/sierra/200511/tr1.asp

Waste Manager
David Baker

It's a dirty job, handling 42,000 tons of trash a year. But, it's not the smell or the filth that bothers David Baker—it's the waste. "You wouldn't believe how much good stuff gets thrown away every day. We get stuff regularly that's still brand new, in the boxes unopened. Money gets thrown out regularly—in couches, in washing machines, in pockets. Sometimes on a windy day the money starts blowing around."

And yes, there are (literally) tons of math involved in being a waste manager.

David questions, "Do you know where your trash goes? Where we live, once a week your family puts the trash out by the curb. Then a garbage truck picks it up and takes it here to the transfer station. But, that's just the beginning.

"At the transfer station, the trash is unloaded into a huge box on a second truck, and the huge box is later put onto a larger truck. Those boxes weigh about 25 tons when full."

1. How many 25-ton boxes do we need to move 42,000 tons of trash every year? (Hint: You don't like dividing by 25? You can divide by 100 and then multiply by 4 instead.)

David continues his explanation: "Now the third truck takes the box full of garbage 42 miles to a rail yard in Centralia, WA. That round trip requires 24 gallons of gas."

2. How many miles per gallon of gas does that truck get?

"At Centralia, the box is loaded onto a railroad car. That train takes the box of garbage 200 miles to Roosevelt, WA, where a landfill is. The train uses 10 gallons of gas per mile when fully loaded, and 0.5 gallons of gas per mile on the return trip," explains David.

3. How many gallons of gas will the train use to haul the garbage from Centralia to Roosevelt including the return trip?

"We're not through yet. Because the tracks don't go all the way to the landfill, the big box of garbage is unloaded from the train to another truck before it finally gets to the landfill, where your garbage is dumped into the ground. The landfill covers 2,000 acres, and the hole is 600 feet deep." One story of a building is about 10 feet.

4. How many stories deep is the landfill?

David poses a good question: "Think about what you buy. It used to be that people kept things for generations. How old are your oldest possessions?"

Soup Kitchen Operator
Ken Benjamin

The food's good and it's hot and it's free. This morning, the menu is whole-grain pancakes, all you can eat, no questions asked. It's open to the poor, the homeless, the hopeless, and the lonely. It's the Community Kitchen. Ken Benjamin began the Community Kitchen in 1988, and he still works here 6 mornings and 2 evenings every week. Ken receives no money from the Community Kitchen, but earns his living landscaping. So why do it?

"Because there is a need," explains Ken. "There are people in this community trying to live off less than $350 a month. The lowest rent you can find is $400 a month, and that doesn't count whatever else you need to get by on, like food. Most of these people are unemployable, for mental or physical reasons. They have nowhere else to go." What's more, the need is growing.

Still, the Community Kitchen has to pay rent, too, as well as gas and water and electricity, which add up to $700 a month. "That's if nothing breaks," Ken laughs. "This is a shoestring operation. We rely on donations. All our food is donated. We never know from one day to the next what ingredients we'll have to cook with."

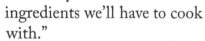

"A lot of people find cooking under those circumstances hard, but if you understand proportions—like the ratio of flour to water to baking powder—you can make it work. The trick is to be able to find the balance. If you understand that balance, you can do anything. That's true in cooking and in life."

© Taylor & Francis Group • *On-the-Job Math Mysteries*

DOI: 10.4324/9781003236924-15

Ken's Secret Pancake Recipe
(feeds 30 people)

2 ½ cups (c.) white flour
14 ounces condensed milk
3 heaping teaspoons (t.) baking powder
2 teaspoon (t.) vanilla
1 ½ cup (c.) whole grain flour
Water until consistency of a smoothie

Stir and pour onto oiled griddle on
medium heat. Turn pancakes when
edges appear dry. Serve onto plate
when both sides are brown.

Ken is anticipating up to 45 people today.

1. So as not to waste any ingredients, how many times the recipe should
   he make?

2. How much of each ingredient are needed?

Raki is one of several volunteers who help to keep the Community
Kitchen open. Right now she is wiping down all surfaces in a solution of 2
tablespoons bleach with 1 gallon of water.

3. If there are 16 tablespoons (T) in a cup, how long will a gallon of
   bleach last?

In order to receive even a small amount of grant money from the government, Ken needs to provide statistics—numerical data about the populations being served. "Today we have 20 people, which includes 12 men and 4 women. The rest are children, 1 boy and 3 girls."

4. What percent of the people being served are men?

5. What percent of the people being served are women?

6. What percent of the people being served are boys?

7. What percent of the people being served are girls?

GREEN DIAMOND RESOURCE COMPANY

Logging Manager
Gerald Barnhart

Douglas fir, hemlock, alder, and cedar trees tower overhead everywhere you look on the Olympic Peninsula. A good portion of that forest land (320,000 acres in Washington State alone) belongs to Green Diamond Resource Company.

"Green Diamond grows trees and sells logs," says Gerald Barnhart, logging manager. "That's important, because wood products are found just about everywhere in life (even toothpaste contains wood cellulose). And, just as wood is found everywhere in life, math is found everywhere in logging.

"We log flat areas using shovel logging, but steep areas require cable logging. Cable logging is expected to produce 6 loads per day, and cost $4,000 per day, while the shovel logging is expected to produce 10 loads per day and cost $1,600 per day."

1. What is the cost per load for each?

"One of our logging trucks weighs 88,000 pounds with its load of alder logs. The truck's tare weight (empty weight) is 30,000 pounds."

2. How much does the load of logs weigh in pounds?

3. How much is that in tons?

"One board foot is 12" long by 12" wide by 1" thick. One log may contain more than 1,000 board feet. We estimate that alder saw logs weigh about 7 tons per thousand board feet (MBF)."

4. How many board feet of lumber is the truck carrying? Round to the nearest hundred.

"Enjoy your time in school. Apply yourself to make the most of it. There's so much to be gained."

Sawmill Operator
Mike Sallee

Mike Sallee's sawmill provides lumber for houses, decks, docks, picture frames, totem poles—you name it. But, Mike doesn't need to cut down any trees for his wood. He finds logs washed up on beaches dislodged by landslides or fierce Alaskan windstorms.

Mike makes all of his deliveries by boat. His sawmill is tucked deep in the Alaskan rainforest, with no roads in any direction. Many of his customers live on remote islands. But, harvesting logs doesn't require math, does it?

Mike disagrees, "I use math all of the time. Especially the Pythagorean Theorem ($a^2 + b^2 = c^2$). Here's an example.

"If I need a 6 inch × 6 inch × 10 foot piece of wood, it's easy to see I need to use a log at least 10 feet long. But how wide does it need to be?"

1. Draw a diagram to show why the log can't be 6 inches in diameter.

Mike continues, "To figure the actual diameter of the log I will need for this board, I use the Pythagorean Theorem: $a^2 + b^2 = c^2$."

Below is a diagram of the cut end of the log, with a and b being the sides we want to cut, and c the width of the log (the diameter.)

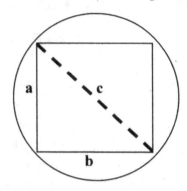

2. Use $a^2 + b^2 = c^2$ to find out the diameter of the log Mike needs to start with. (Round up to the nearest inch.)

"The local museum needs 14 pieces of yellow cedar for the sides of some bentwood boxes they're making. They need each piece to be 6 feet long by 12 inches wide by 1 inch thick. I charge by the board foot of lumber. One board foot is one foot long by one foot wide by one inch thick. To find board feet, multiply length (in feet) × width (in feet) × thickness (in inches)."

3. How many board feet of yellow cedar do they want altogether?

4. If Mike charges $1.10 per board foot, how much should he bill the museum for 14 boards? Add $0.10 per board foot for delivery.

Mike is happy with his life. "I like making something productive out of logs that would just rot on the beach."

Commercial Fisherman
Rudy Johanson

Commercial fishing is one of the deadliest occupations on earth. In the coastal waters of Alaska, fishing boats are sometimes tossed around by waves 50 feet tall. Rudy Johanson has been working as a commercial fisherman since he was 12 years old. His father was a commercial fisherman, and his grandfather owned a salmon cannery. Rudy's Tlingit ancestors also were fishermen.

Is math needed for fishing? You bet.

Rudy describes, "I take the boat out to a likely spot in the ocean. Then a crewmember in a skiff circles the fish with a net, and the net is hauled on board. Fish come pouring down onto the back deck—pink salmon, chum, sockeye, coho, rockfish, red snapper, and black cod. Sometimes just one fish can weigh hundreds of pounds. That's a lot of weight for the Prospector to hold.

"Each time we pull in the net, it's called a set. A good set averages 4,000 to 5,000 pounds. A really good set can take in more than 15,000 pounds of fish."

Rudi built the Prospector in the 1970s. "I can't remember how many boats I've built over the years."

1. The boat holds 75,000 pounds of fish. How many 5,000-pound sets would it take to fill the boat?

2. How many 15,000-pound sets would it take to fill the boat?

DOI: 10.4324/9781003236924-18

"One day the boat was full in four hours of fishing."

3. 78,000 pounds of pink salmon averages to be 26,000 fish. What is the average weight of each pink salmon brought on board?

Don't worry! Rudy's not catching all of the salmon in the sea. Fishing is strictly regulated to make sure the species survive and prosper. "In the 1950s, we took in 150,000 pounds for the whole season. Those were lean times. Nowadays, the fleet catches 1,000,000 pounds of fish a season."

4. How many times more fish does Rudy catch today than 50 years ago?

The weight of all of those fish often sends water pouring over the rail of the boat, but the boats can take it. Even so, Rudy and his crew try to avoid bad weather. "We have been out in some scary stuff. Once we were out in 80 mile-per-hour winds. It's a lot nicer to anchor somewhere safe and wait it out.

"We deal with the tides a lot," says Rudy. "We get anywhere from a 19-foot high to a negative 4-foot low tide around here. So, you're talking about a huge wall of water moving in or out every 6 hours."

5. What is the difference in feet between a 19-foot and a negative 4-foot tide?

Rudy notes, "Tides are real important when we go after halibut, a fish with both eyes on the same side of its head. The crew anchors longlines set with 100 hooks onto the ocean bottom, and then we sail off to set more lines elsewhere."

"Here's the tricky part. If we stay out too long and can't find our way back to that exact spot in time (there are no road maps in the ocean), the tide will drag the anchors, and then the longlines can break. If the longlines break, we lose all of our fish, our anchor, our hooks, and all of our hard work. It's even more challenging in a dense fog.

"We anchor our longlines up to 300 fathoms deep. One fathom is the same as 6 feet."

6. How deep can Rudy and the crew set their longlines in feet?

According to Rudy, "The largest halibut I ever caught weighed 280 pounds."

7. How many times larger was the halibut than a 100-pound student?

"When we pull into port after halibut fishing, the National Marine Fisheries Board is right there to weigh our catch. There's a fine for catching more than our 20,000-pound per season quota."

How does Rudy know the weight of all the fish on board? He adds them up in his head. As each halibut is pulled on board, a crewmember measures its length and shouts that number up to Rudy in the wheelhouse. Rudy uses the chart provided to determine the gross weight of each fish. He adds up the weight of each fish in his head . . .while he's driving the boat!

"Sometimes in the net we find a ratfish, an eel, or an octopus or two. Lots of stinging jellyfish."

8. Pair up with a partner, or work as a class on this next activity. As a group, come up with a name for your own fishing boat. Then, designate one person to call out the lengths of each halibut (see the list of lengths below), while another person writes down these lengths and converts them to pounds using the Halibut Length/Weight Table. You can make this a contest to see who can calculate the total weight of all of the ship's catch the quickest! What is the total weight of your ship's catch?

Lengths of each halibut fish (in inches):
33, 45, 55, 38, 70, 44, 39, 44, 45, 60, 59, 39, 66, 44, 43, 37, 44, 38, 55, 52, 68, 48, 54, 77, 40, 33, 43, 55, 44, 64, 45, 55, 38, 54.

Halibut Length/Weight Table			
Length (inches)	Weight	Length (inches)	Weight
32	12	56	76
33	14	57	80
34	15	58	85
35	17	59	90
36	18	60	95
37	20	61	100
38	22	62	106
39	24	63	111
40	26	64	117
41	28	65	123
42	30	66	129
43	32	67	136
44	35	68	142
45	37	69	149
46	40	70	156
47	43	71	164
48	46	72	171
49	49	73	179
50	53	74	187
51	56	75	196
52	60	76	204
53	63	77	213
54	67	78	222
55	72	79	231

Now try this again as a class, checking the chart, but adding it up in your head, as Rudy does. Easy to make a mistake? Try driving a boat at the same time!

Extension

Are halibut longer than their weight, or heavier than their length? Use the information from the Halibut Length/Weight Table to draw a line graph that illustrates this relationship. Use graph paper, and remember to label the horizontal (x) and vertical (y) axes. Draw a diagonal to show where the equal length and weight appear on the graph. Then, give your graph a title.

Canning factories pay Rudy for his catch. The price varies from season to season, but currently he receives the following:

Pink salmon. . . . .$0.11 per pound
Sockeye salmon . . . .$0.75 per pound
Chum salmon . . . .$0.25 per pound
Large halibut (60#+) . . . .$3.00 per pound
Medium halibut (40# +) . . . .$2.80 per pound
Small halibut (Less than 40#) . . . . .$2.60 per pound

The symbol # can stand for "pound" as well as "number."

9. How much more will Rudy get for a 60# halibut than a 59# halibut? (Hint: The answer is not 20 cents.)

10. How much more will Rudy get for a 40# halibut than a 39# halibut?

11. How much money will he receive for a full-season's quota of halibut if all of the halibut are medium-sized?

"A long time ago everything was done by hand. We rowed out and set the nets by hand. Today it's all done with hydraulics and power. We're catching more fish, but making less money than we did then."

Salmon prices weren't always low. The introduction of salmon farming in pens has made salmon much cheaper to produce. With a bigger supply of salmon available, there is less demand for Rudy's wild-caught salmon. Because there is less demand, the price Rudy gets is lower.

12. A 1-pound can of wild pink salmon costs $3.40 in the grocery store. How much of that money goes to Rudy?

After Rudy pays his crew, pays his taxes, pays his harbor permit, buys his halibut license, pays for the upkeep and maintenance on his boat, buys his fuel for each trip, and pays for all of the other expenses involved with fishing, he's not getting rich. However, being rich isn't all that important to Rudy Johanson. "I enjoy fishing immensely."

"I figure I make about the same as a waitress. But I wouldn't trade my life for anything."

Air Traffic Controller
Roger McDonald

The air around Ketchikan, Alaska, swarms with helicopters, private jets, commercial jets, military aircraft, and float planes. Air traffic controller Roger McDonald watches it all from his high glass tower, directing as many as 700 planes a day. Roger is responsible for each one of those planes—he can't afford to make a mistake.

According to Roger, a Cessna flies at 120 miles per hour.

1. How many miles is that per minute?

To avoid confusing a.m. and p.m., pilots and air traffic controllers use a 24-hour clock. For example, according to this system, 7 p.m. is written as 1900 (pronounced "nineteen hundred") because 7 p.m. is the 19th hour of the day.

2. What time is your school day over, using 24-hour time?

"Pilots travel at great speeds, and travel through many different time zones. You can imagine the confusion that could happen when a pilot calls in her ETA (estimated time of arrival). Which time zone is she talking about? Well, that's why it was agreed that everyone should use the time right now in England, and we call that universal time.

"If the universal time clock shows that it's almost 1900 (nineteen hundred) right now in England, it's noon here in Alaska."

3. Does the sun come up earlier or later in England, and how many hours' difference is there?

4. What time is your school day over, in universal time? (You may need to consult a map.)

Roger shares a typical problem (he figures it in his head, but you might want to use paper): "It really gets crazy in here sometimes, but I'll give you an easy one. Universal time is 0900 ("oh-900")."

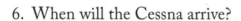

Roger says, "Accidents result from bad calculations."

Three aircraft are flying toward the airport (inbound):

- 5 miles west of the airport is a Piper Cub flying 60 mph.
- Behind him, 10 miles west of the airport is a Cessna flying 120 mph.
- 20 miles east of the airport, is a big Alaska Airlines jet flying 240 mph.

5. When will the Piper Cub arrive?

6. When will the Cessna arrive?

7. When will the Alaska Airlines jet arrive?

Part of Roger's job is to watch for bears and deer on the runway, and to warn float plane pilots of whales in the water. (You don't want to bring your plane down on an 8-ton orca.) Eagles can be a problem too. "If a 10-pound eagle hits a 160,000-pound Boeing 737, you can guess who wins," he says. But, planes sometimes have to land after hitting an eagle.

Talk Like an Air Traffic Controller

The letter P sounds a lot like B, and many other letters sound very much alike. To prevent confusion, pilots use the international alphabet shown below. For example, if your airplane is FQ 147, you identify yourself as Foxtrot Quebec 147. What are your initials?

Alpha	November
Bravo	Oscar
Charlie	Papa
Delta	Quebec
Echo	Romeo
Foxtrot	Sierra
Golf	Tango
Hotel	Uniform
India	Victor
Juliett	Whiskey
Kilo	X-ray
Lima	Yankee
Mike	Zulu

Check out the National Air Traffic Controllers Association Web site to see a map of all of the planes flying over the U.S. right now (http://www. natca.org/flight-explorer/united-states.aspx).

Master Carver
Nathan Jackson

Nathan Jackson can be a little grumpy at times, but you might be a little grumpy too if you had tourists continually surrounding you, snapping photos and asking questions. You see, Nathan Jackson is one of the world's premier totem pole carvers (he was named a "living cultural treasure" by the United States National Endowment for the Arts), and people flock to see him work.

Nathan wasn't always a carver. For much of his life, he was a fisherman. It wasn't until he got deathly sick that Nathan found his true calling in life as a carver. Recovering in bed from pneumonia, Nathan began whittling. In a few weeks, when he had a display case full of miniature totem poles, he realized that he had the gift for carving. Nathan wanted his carving to be more than just the making of tourist souvenirs.

He wanted to continue the deep and meaningful carving traditions of his Tlingit ancestors, so Nathan began a careful study of their traditional forms. Now Nathan replicates those forms as faithfully as possible, and his works seem to echo the songs of those ancient Native peoples.

Traditionally, Native people made paint by chewing salmon eggs and then mixing the paste with pulverized rock of many colors.

© Taylor & Francis Group • *On-the-Job Math Mysteries*

51

DOI: 10.4324/9781003236924-20

1. The first step for a carver is to design the image that will adorn the pole. He creates a drawing and then a blueprint to scale of the imagined pole. The drawing usually is on a scale of 1 inch to 1 foot. Nathan's blueprint for "Opening the Box of Wisdom" shows the pole 2 ½ feet high. How tall will the finished totem pole really be?

2. The next step is to select the perfect tree. The red cedar Nathan chose to become the "Opening the Box of Wisdom" pole stood about 4 feet in diameter. Every inch signifies about 10 years of growth. How old was this tree when it was cut? What was life like in America the year this tree first started to grow?

> Live cedar trees in Southeast Alaska are sometimes more than 1,000 years old.

3. The tree was very heavy. One cubic foot (one foot tall by one foot wide by one foot deep) of red cedar weighs 27 pounds when still wet. That same cubic foot will weigh about 23 pounds when it dries out. After the branches were removed, the log contained about 1,500 cubic feet of wood. How much did this pole weigh wet? Give answer in pounds and tons.

4. How much less will the log weigh when it dries?

5. After removing the bark, the carver must shave down 3" through the sappy, sticky outer layer to the good carving wood. If the downed log was 4 feet in diameter and its bark was 2 inches thick, what was the diameter of the log after removing the bark and sapwood?

6. The 30-foot totem Nathan is working on in the photo was begun June 1 of last year and is scheduled for completion June 21 of this year. About how many weeks is that?

Nathan now has more than 30 years of carving experience, and his poles stand in cities around the world, commissioned by museums and universities, parks and historic sites, and sometimes by families. Want a totem pole in your yard? It will cost you.

Traditionally, carvers used clam shells, hard rocks like jade and obsidian, and sometimes beaver's teeth to dig out the wood.

7. The cost of a pole depends on the experience of the carver. Less-experienced carvers receive $1,000 a foot; more-experienced carvers like Nathan command $3,000 a foot or more. Suppose the contract agreement states that the carver will be paid $3,150 per foot, and the finished pole will be 30 feet tall. What will be the carver's pay (not counting the cost of tools, paint, workspace, utilities, postage, shipping, and taxes)?

8. 15% of the total price will be taken in taxes. How much will the carver receive in total after taxes?

9. The world's largest authentic totem pole is in Kake, Alaska, and measures 162 ½ feet high. How many times taller is this totem pole than a 5-foot tall person?

10. One of the world's largest totem poles has a diameter of 14 1/2 feet. The circumference (the distance around the trunk) is always about 3 times larger than the diameter (distance across). Using these figures, what is the distance around the totem pole?

11. How many kids in your class would it take to hold hands around that pole?

Check me out on the Web: http://www. alaskatrekker.com/carving_video.htm

Diver
Hans Hjort

Alaska Commercial Divers, Inc.

It's a dangerous job—freezing water, heavy equipment, attacking sharks, stinging jellyfish, intimidating sea lions, electrical shocks, and much more. Commercial divers like Hans Hjort work underwater, salvaging sunken boats, repairing ship hulls, and looking for lost treasure.

Hans learned to scuba dive when he was 14, and started working as a diver when he was 17. Now he is the manager of Alaska Commercial Divers. "I was never that good at math until I went to dive school. Then it became interesting. There's a lot of math and physics involved in diving. Here are some examples:

"Right now I'm measuring the thickness of steel on a Coast Guard ship. If any part of the hull has rusted to less than ⅛ inch thick, it will have to be replaced. My probe shows the thinnest area is 0.122 inches.

1. Does the hull need to be replaced?

Hans continues, "Another cool tool we use is an underwater cutting torch. It can cut through steel, rock, and even cement. The torch needs 90 pounds of air in order to burn on land. Underwater, where the pressure is higher, the torch needs even more air. (You may have felt this pressure on your ears when you were swimming.) There's an increase of about 0.5 pound of pressure for every foot you go down. Well, for this job, I'm going down 50 feet."

2. How many pounds of air pressure will I need in order to use the torch?

© Taylor & Francis Group • *On-the-Job Math Mysteries*
55
DOI: 10.4324/9781003236924-21

"When doing something involving the ocean, you need to know what the tides are doing. An example would be if you plan to camp on an ocean beach—check the local tide table. The water might be way out when you set up your tent, but just a few hours later it could be lapping at your tent door. The water depth might go up and down 20 feet in just 6 hours (like it does some days in Ketchikan). Fortunately, tides are very predictable, thanks to mathematics, so all we have to do is consult a tide table to know how high and how low the tides will be, and when they occur."

Tide Table for Ketchikan, Alaska

Date	High Tide	Low Tide	High Tide	Low Tide
Wednesday, Nov. 14	03:13 a.m. 12.7 Ft	08:35 a.m. 5.5 Ft	02:32 p.m. 14.6 Ft	09:18 p.m. 0.8 Ft
Thursday, Nov. 15	04:00 a.m. 12.3 Ft	09:21 a.m. 6.1 Ft	03:16 p.m. 14.0 Ft	10:06 p.m. 1.5 Ft
Friday, Nov. 16	04:54 a.m. 12.1 Ft	10:20 a.m. 6.4 Ft	04:21 p.m. 12.6 Ft	11:01 p.m. 2.1 Ft
Saturday, Nov. 17	05:55 a.m. 12.8 Ft	11:35 a.m. 6.3 Ft	05:22 p.m. 12.6 Ft	12:00 mid. 2.5 Ft

3. Use the information on the Tide Table above to graph the height of the water as it rises and falls from Thursday morning through Friday evening.

Ketchikan Tide Levels

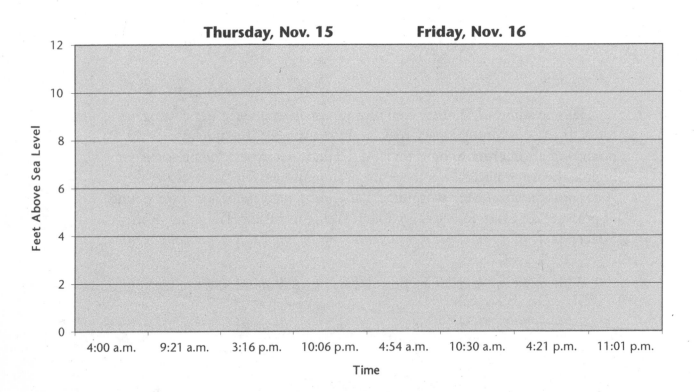

According to Hans, "Everything underwater is more difficult. Something that would be really easy on the surface can become a huge challenge underwater—like hooking up a pipe, changing propellers, and finding anything you drop underwater.

"Last summer, a cruise ship lost an 8-ton anchor right off the dock in 90 feet of water. Because of the pressure, a diver can only stay down for 20 minutes at that depth. The anchor had sunk beneath the mud, and it took me 3 full dives to find it. It took me another full dive to recover it. We charge $420 per hour of diving, figured to the nearest minute."

4. How much did Hans and his crew charge for that job?

"A full balloon at the surface contains 79% Nitrogen and 21% Oxygen. The percent stays the same at depth, but the balloon gets smaller because the water pressure compresses the air. At 33 feet, the balloon is ½ the size. At 66 feet, it is ¼ of its original size. Unlike the balloon, your lungs underwater don't shrink; they just take in more air to feel full. That means that at 33 feet, they are taking in twice the air. Your body can't take that much nitrogen in your bloodstream for long, which is why we can't stay down long.

"If your lungs were 100% full at 33 feet and you came to the surface without exhaling, they could burst. That's why divers have to come up slowly—30 feet per minute. No faster."

5. If I dive to 90 feet of water at 11:41 a.m., and have to be back to the surface by 12:01 p.m., when is the latest I should start for the surface?

Hans' job can be very exciting. "Once I caught a 25-pound halibut by its tail. It would have made a good dinner, but I only had so much time left underwater, and in order to finish the job I was doing, I had to let it go." However, he also sees another side to it: "It's a dangerous job. Once I was called upon to recover the body of another diver who wasn't so lucky. This stuff happens. You never know when." When asked to name the best thing about his job, he answers, "The best thing about my job? There's always something new. We never do the same thing twice."

Bush Pilot
Michelle Masden

Michelle Masden takes passengers soaring over the jagged green islands of the Alexander Archipelago. Some of her passengers are fishermen, looking for runs of salmon or herring. Sometimes her passengers are tourists—straining out the windows—hoping to catch sight of mountain goats, wolves, or brown bear.

"A lot of my flying is spent helping the Alaska Department of Fish and Game track wolves. As we fly over an area, they listen for a signal given off by radio collars on the wild wolves.

"When we're heading out wolf tracking, I have no idea how long it will take, and I sure don't want to run out of fuel. My Cessna 185 floatplane holds 78 gallons of fuel. At normal cruising speed, it burns 17 gallons of fuel per hour."

1. How many hours will I be able to fly? Find to the nearest tenth.

2. Convert that to hours and minutes.

"Math—there's lots of it in my job. You use it so much it becomes automatic."

"The FAA (Federal Aviation Administration) wisely requires that I keep a 30-minute reserve in my tank. (I would anyway.)"

3. How much time does Michelle have to fly given that requirement?

"Most of the radio tracking is done on Prince of Wales Island, 25 miles from my home. The airplane flies at 120 miles per hour cruising speed."

4. How many hours of flying time will it take Michelle to get to Prince of Wales and back? Find to nearest tenth.

5. Convert that to hours and minutes.

6. How much time can Michelle spend radio tracking once she get to Prices of Wales Island? (Find answer in hours and minutes.)

"When there's a headwind, the plane can be traveling at cruise air speed, but compared to the ground, it may really be going only half that speed. For example, if I keep the engine at its optimum airspeed of 120 miles per hour, but I am flying straight into a 40-mile-per-hour headwind, my ground speed will only be 80 miles per hour."

7. How long will the 25-mile trip back from Prince of Wales take against a 40-mile per hour wind? Find the answer to one decimal place and then convert to hours and minutes.

8. How long will the trip take against a 60-mile per hour wind?

9. How long will it take with a 20-mile per hour wind at her back? (Find answer in hours and minutes.)

Michelle explains, "My Cessna 185 has a payload of 1,200 total pounds. After you subtract my weight, it can hold 1,060 pounds. A gallon of fuel weighs 6 pounds."

10. With a full tank of gas, how many pounds of tourists can Michelle carry?

Michelle poses this problem: "Three tourists would like me to take them flightseeing. There is a grandmother who weighs 210 pounds including her handbag; a man with binoculars and camera, whose total weight is 226 pounds; and a woman weighing 179 pounds. I have three passenger seats."

11. Can Michelle take all three of them flightseeing?

"I can take more tourists if I carry less than a full tank of fuel. A sightseeing trip into Misty Fjords National Monument takes 1.25 hours round trip."

12. Assuming there is no wind, what is the minimum amount of gas she needs to travel there and back at normal cruising speed?

13. Could Michelle take the three tourists to Misty Fjords National Monument and back if I take only the minimum required gas? (Assume there is no wind.)

Name:_____ Date:_____

When asked when she decided to become a pilot, Michelle responds, "I was one of those kids who just fell in love with flying. I was writing poetry about it in third grade. I used to take the bus out to watch the planes take off and land. On my 16th birthday I took my first private flying lesson. At that time, private lessons cost $30 an hour. I scraped together the money by working several jobs—at the House of Pies, Burger King, babysitting—and on my 17th birthday, I received my private pilot's license.

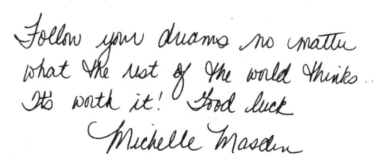

"I don't take chances," Michelle continues. "When the weather starts deteriorating, I turn around. Things can happen really fast in an airplane. You have to be able to react instantly.

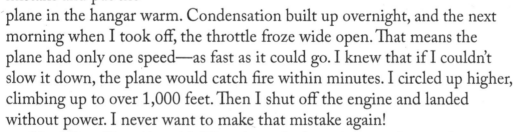

"Once I made a mistake and put the plane in the hangar warm. Condensation built up overnight, and the next morning when I took off, the throttle froze wide open. That means the plane had only one speed—as fast as it could go. I knew that if I couldn't slow it down, the plane would catch fire within minutes. I circled up higher, climbing up to over 1,000 feet. Then I shut off the engine and landed without power. I never want to make that mistake again!

"As Albert Einstein said, 'Experience is the name people give their mistakes.'"

Follow your dreams no matter what the rest of the world thinks. Its worth it! Good luck

Michelle Masden

Circus Performers (pp. 1–4)

Ringmaster
1. $(57 \times 2) + (47 \times 3) =$
114 + 141 = at least 255 feet wide

Elephant Trainer
2. 7,500 pounds ÷ 100 = 75
75 × 1.25 = 93.75 pounds of vitamins

3. 7,500 pounds ÷ 100 = 75
75 × 1.25 = 93.75 pounds of vitamins

4. 8,500 pounds ÷ 100 = 85
85 × 1.25 = 106.25 pounds of vitamins

High Wire Acrobat
5. 25 feet ÷ 10 feet = 2.5 or 2 ½ stories high

Organic Farmer (pp. 5–7)
1. 43,560 cubic feet ÷ 12 inches per foot = 3,630 cubic feet of water

2. 1 cubic foot = 7.5 gallons
3,630 cubic feet = 7.5 × 3,630 = 27,225 gallons

Total Amount Picked (lb = pound)	Smallest Possible Share	Each Share	Leftovers
57 zucchinis	Figure to the nearest whole zucchini	57 divided by 18 = 3 r 3 **3 zucchinis**	18 × 3 = 54 57 − 54 = 3 **3 zucchinis**
100 tomatoes	Figure to the nearest whole tomato	100 divided by 18 = 5 r 10 **5 tomatoes**	18 × 5 = 90 100 − 90 = 10 **10 tomatoes**
39 lb of rhubarb	Figure to the nearest lb	39 divided by 18 = 2 r 3 **2 lb rhubarb**	2 × 18 = 36 39 − 36 = 3 **3 lb rhubarb**
3 gallons of blackberries	Figure to the nearest pint	2 pints = 1 quart 4 quarts = 1 gallon 8 pints = 1 gallon 8 × 3 = 24 gallons 24 divided by 18 = 1 r 6 **1 pint berries**	1 pint × 18 = 18 24 − 18 = 6 **6 pints blackberries**
5 gallons of peas (5 lb per gallon)	Figure to the nearest lb	5 gallons × 5 lb = 25 lb 25 divided by 18 = 1 r 7 **1 lb peas**	1 × 18 = 18 25 − 18 = 7 **7 lb peas**
58 dahlias	Figure to the nearest flower	58 divided by 18 = 3 r 4 **3 flowers**	3 × 18 = 54 58 − 54 = 4 **4 flowers**
5 lb of basil	Figure to the nearest ¼ lb bunch	5 divided by ¼ = 20 bunches 20 divided by 18 = 1 r 2 **¼ lb or 1 bunch of basil**	¼ × 18 = ¹⁸⁄₄ = 4 ¾ = 4 ½ 5 − 4 ½ = ½ lb **½ lb of basil or 2 bunches**
9 lb of kale	Figure to the nearest ½ lb	9 lb divided by 18 = ½ lb of kale (one bunch)	None
12 lb of beet greens	Figure to the nearest ½ lb	12 divided by 18 = ⅔, which is a little more than **½ lb greens** (one bunch)	½ × 18 = 9 12 − 9 = 3 **3 lb greens (6 bunches)**

Dogsled Musher (pp. 8–10)

1. 1,200 miles long divided by 120 miles per day = 10 days

2. 80 degrees below zero plus 68 degrees above zero = 148 degrees colder

3. $\dfrac{10,000}{2,500} = \dfrac{100}{25} =$ 4 times more

   2 dishes times 4 = 8 dishes per day

4. There are 4 cups/quart, and 4 quarts/gallon, so that makes 16 cups/gallon: 16 cups per dog.

5. 16 cups × 16 dogs = 256

6.
	19	24	
1973	~~20~~ days	~~0~~ hours	49 minutes
Ray	9 days	21 hours	26 minutes
	10 days	3 hours	23 minutes faster

Beekeepers (pp. 11–12)

1. 50 colonies × 100 pounds = 5,000 pounds

2. (50 × 300) – (50 × 100 pounds) = 15,000 pounds – 5,000 pounds = 10,000 pounds more

3. 5,000 ÷ 640 = more than 7, so we need 8 barrels.

4. Water:
   1 gallon = 4 quarts
   1 quart = 2 pints
   Therefore, 1 gallon = 8 pints
   8 pounds ÷ 8 pints = 1 pound per pint
   Therefore, water weighs 16 ounces per pint. Honey vs. Water:
   22 ounces – 16 ounces = 6 ounces heavier

5. ¼ pound of bees to provide for each queen × 84 queen cells = 21 pounds of nurse bees

Kayak Guide (pp. 13–14)

1. *Trip #1*
   2 triple kayaks, 3 double kayaks, 2 single kayaks
   2 guides needed

2. *Trip #2*
   2 triple kayaks, 3 double kayaks, 1 single kayak
   2 guides needed

3. *Trip #3*
   2 triple kayaks, 1 double kayak, 1 single kayak
   2 guides needed

4. 63 (If you got 50 energy bars, you forgot to pack any for Gillian.)

5. 3 miles in one hour
   1 mile in (60 minutes divided by 3) = 20 minutes
   2 miles = 40 minutes
   5 miles = 1 hour and 40 minutes

6. 4 miles in 1 hour
   1 mile in (60 minutes divided by 4) = 15 minutes
   5 miles = 1 hour and 15 minutes

7. Total Time needed (in minutes)

Guide prepares breakfast, strikes tent	45
Group eats breakfast	30
Strike camp and pack kayaks	60
Paddling time to Grace Creek	75
	210

210 ÷ 60 = 3 hours 30 minutes = 3 ½ hours
11:34 − 3:30 = 8:04 a.m. (That's sleeping in for them!)

Shellfish Farmer (pp. 15–16)

1. 7 gallons ÷ 2 = 3.5 gallons or 3 ½ gallons per hour

2. 60 minutes per hour × 3 hours = 180 minutes
   180 minutes ÷ 9 minutes per bucket = 20 buckets

3. 100 socks × 30 pounds = 3,000 pounds of clams

4. 3,000 × 22 = 66,000 clams every 2 weeks

5. 52 weeks in a year ÷ 2 = 26
   66,000 clams × 26 = 1,716,000 clams a year

6. 1,716,000 × 13 = 22,308,000
   1,716,000 ÷ 2 = 858,800
   22,308,000 + 858,800 = 23,166,000 clams

County Judge (pp. 17–18)

1. $\dfrac{2}{3} = \dfrac{20}{30}$ 20 is ⅔ of 30. Therefore, she should be given a 30-day sentence.

2. ⅓ of 45 = 15 days off for good time
   45 − 15 = 30 days need to be served
   30 − 16 days already served = 14 days more in jail

3. 45 + 90 = 135

4. 365 − 135 days minimum = 230 days less than the maximum sentence

Railroad Engineer (pp. 19–21)

1. 13

2. 17

3. Not 23 ½. (Dave would be in a lot of trouble if he split a rail car in half.) The answer is 23 or 24.

4. 26 + 7 + 12 = 45 cars

5.
Load	1 hour	60 minutes
Trip to mill	10 miles/15 miles per hour = 40/60 =	40 minutes
Swap string	20 minutes	20 minutes
Empty back	20 minutes	20 minutes
	140 minutes = 2 hours and 20 minutes	

6.
Load	1 ½ hours	1 hour 30 minutes
Trip to mill	10 miles @ 10 miles per hour	1 hour
Double the hills		30 minutes
Swap string		20 minutes
Full back		1 hour 10 minutes
	3 hours and 90 minutes = 4 hours and 30 minutes	

Videographer (pp. 22–23)

1.
Video camera	896	grams
Tripod	2,800	grams
Telephoto lens	112	grams
Wide angle lens	84	grams
Batteries 5 × 126 =	630	grams
Solar Charger	196	grams
Mini tapes 10 × 28 =	280	grams
Microphone	56	grams
Camera bag	98	grams
Camera equipment	5,152	grams

5.2 kilograms camera equipment
+15.5 kilograms gear and food
20.7 kilograms total

2. 17 batteries × 126 grams each = 2,142 grams

5 batteries = 630 grams
Solar charger = 196 grams
826 grams

2,142 grams
− 826 grams
1,316 grams (almost 3 pounds!)

3.

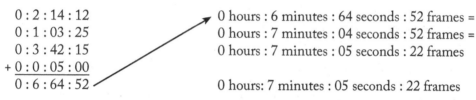

0 : 2 : 14 : 12 $\qquad$ 0 hours : 6 minutes : 64 seconds : 52 frames =
0 : 1 : 03 : 25 $\qquad$ 0 hours : 7 minutes : 04 seconds : 52 frames =
0 : 3 : 42 : 15 $\qquad$ 0 hours : 7 minutes : 05 seconds : 22 frames
+ 0 : 0 : 05 : 00
0 : 6 : 64 : 52 $\qquad$ 0 hours: 7 minutes : 05 seconds : 22 frames

4. $\qquad$ Music 7 minutes : 18 seconds : 00 frames
Video 7 minutes : 05 seconds : 22 frames

Which is the same as:
Music 7 minutes : 17 seconds : 30 frames
Video 7 minutes : 05 seconds : 22 frames
12 seconds : 08 frames

Heavy Equipment Operator (pp. 24–25)

1. 1 hour = 60 minutes
   60 minutes ÷ 10 minutes = 6 loads

2. 6 loads × 8 hours = 48

3. 2 × 20 minutes = 40 minutes = 4 dump truck loads
   48 loads − 4 loads = 44 loads

4. 44 × 6 = 264

5. 10 minutes = 1 load
   1 load × 2 drivers = 2 loads
   264 loads − 2 loads = 262 loads

6. 1 yard = 3 feet
   3 feet × 3 feet × 3 feet = 27 feet

7. 15 × ¾ = $^{45}/_4$ = 11 ¼ tons

8. 11 ¼ tons × 44 loads =
    11 × 44 = 484
    ¼ × 44 = 11
    484 + 11 = 495

Wildlife Veterinary Tech (pp. 26–27)

1. 1 hour until midnight and then 12 more = 13 hours

2. 50 × 0.30 = 15 pounds of food

3. clams, squid, crab, and mussels = 4 parts
    15 ÷ 4 = 3.75 pounds or 3 ¾ pounds

4. 24 ÷ 3 = 8 times

5. 3.75 pounds per day ÷ 8 = 0.47 pounds
    or 3 ¾ ÷ 8 = $^{15}/_4$ ÷ 8 = $^{15}/_4$ × ⅛ = $^{15}/_{32}$ (about a half pound)

6. 35mL per kg × 22 kg = 770 mL

7. 23 beats every 15 seconds

    $$\frac{23 \text{ beats}}{15 \text{ seconds}} = \frac{x \text{ beats}}{60 \text{ seconds}}$$

    Because 4 × 15 = 60, multiply 23 × 4.
    23 × 4 = 92 beats per minute

8. 230 × 3 = 690 days (less than 2 years)

Software Engineer (pp. 28–30)

1. There are three possible solutions: DFACEB, ADFCEB, or ACDFEB.

2. DFACEB, ADFCEB, ACDFEB

3. In order to be divisible by 6, a number must be divisible by both 3 and by 2. If it is divisible by 3 and by 2, it will be divisible by 6. Therefore, if we can prove in-betweens are divisible by 3 and by 2, we are done.

    Prime numbers are always odd (except 2). In-betweens are between prime numbers; therefore, in-betweens have to be even, which means they have to be divisible by 2.

    In-betweens are between two prime numbers. Together, they make up three numbers in a row. The prime numbers cannot be divisible by 3 or they would not be prime. Every third whole number is divisible by 3. Therefore, one of the numbers must be divisible by 3. Therefore, the in-between is divisible by 3. Four is the exception, because it is between 3 and 5; it is divisible by 2, but it is not divisible by 3.

Environmental Health Specialist (pp. 31–32)

1. 8 × 7 = 56 pounds

2. 8 pounds × 30.5 = 244 pounds

3. 8 × 365 = 2,920 (2,928 in a leap year)

4. 2,920 × 10 = 29,200 pounds

5. 5 feet tall × 20 feet wide × 27 feet long = 2,700 cubic feet

6. 2,700 cubic feet ÷ 27 cubic feet per yard = 100 yards

7. Yes
    100 cubic yards × 10 tires per cubic yard = 1,000 tires

Waste Manager (pp. 33–34)

1. 42,000 tons ÷ 25 tons per box = 1,680 boxes

2. 42 miles × 2 ways = 84 miles
   84 miles ÷ 24 gallons = 3.5 miles per gallon

3. 10 × 200 = 2,000 gallons one way
   0.5 × 200 = 100 gallons return
   2,000 + 100 = 2,100 gallons of gas

4. 600 feet ÷ 10 = 60 stories deep

Soup Kitchen Operator (pp. 35–37)

1. 45 people ÷ 30 people = $^{45}/_{30}$ = 1 ½ times

2. 2 ½ cups (c.) white flour × 1 ½ = $^5/_2$ × $^3/_2$ = $^{15}/_4$ = 3 ¾ cups white flour
   14 ounces condensed milk × 1 ½ = 14 + 7 = 21 ounces milk
   3 heaping teaspoons (t.) baking powder × 1 ½ = 4 ½ cups baking powder
   2 teaspoon (t.) vanilla × 1 ½ = 2 + 1 = 3 teaspoons vanilla
   1 ½ cup (c.) whole grain flour × 1 ½ = $^3/_2$ × $^3/_2$ = $^9/_4$ = 2 ¼ cups whole grain flour

3. 16 T = 1 cup
   1 gallon = 4 quarts = 16 cups
   16 cups × 16 T = 256 T.
   There are 256 T in one gallon
   We use 2 tablespoons (T) of bleach in 1 gallon of water
   256 T ÷ 2 T. = 128 uses

4. 12 out of 20 = $^{12}/_{20}$ = $^3/_5$ = $^{60}/_{100}$ = 60% men

5. 4 out of 20 = $^4/_{20}$ = $^1/_5$ = $^{20}/_{100}$ = 20% women

6. 1 out of 20 = $^1/_{20}$ = $^5/_{100}$ = 5% boys

7. 3 out of 20 = $^3/_{20}$ = $^{15}/_{100}$ = 15% girls

Logging Manager (pp. 38–39)

1. 4,000 ÷ 6 = $667 per load (rounded)
   1,600)10 = $160 per load

2.   88,000
    − 30,000
      58,000 pounds

3. 58,000 ÷ 2,000 = 29 tons

4. $\dfrac{7\ tons}{1000\ board\ feet} = \dfrac{29\ tons}{x\ board\ feet}$
   7x = 29,000
   x = 4,143 board feet ≈ 4,100 board feet

Sawmill Operator (pp. 40–41)

1. As shown here, the diagonal is longer than either of the sides of a square. It has to be this way. (Try drawing a square in which the diagonal is shorter than the sides, and you'll see why.) If your diagram explains why, even if it doesn't look like this, it's right.

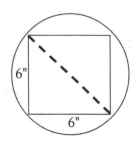

2.

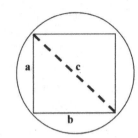

$a^2 + b^2 = c^2$
$6^2 + 6^2 = c^2$
$36 + 36 = c^2$
$72 = c^2$
What does c equal?
$8 \times 8 = 64$
$9 \times 9 = 81$
So, c is between 8 and 9. Therefore, the tree needs to be 9 inches wide.

3. 6' × 1' × 1" = 6 board feet
   6 board feet × 14 boards = 84 board feet

4. $1.10 $1.00 × 6 = $6.00
   + .10 $0.20 × 6 = $1.20
   ‾‾‾‾‾   ‾‾‾‾‾‾‾‾‾‾‾‾‾‾‾‾‾‾
   $1.20 $7.20 per board

   $7.20
   × 14
   ‾‾‾‾‾
   2 8 8 0
   720
   ‾‾‾‾‾
   $100.80 for all

Commercial Fisherman (pp. 42–47)

1. 15

2. 5

3. 3

4. 150,000 pounds/1,000,000 pounds
   We are looking for the number of fish now compared with number of fish back then, so we divide number of fish now by number fish back then:
   1,000,000/150,000 = 6.66666 ≈ 6.7 or 6 ⅔ times more fish.

5. 19 − (-4) = 19 + 4 = 23 feet

6. 1 fathom = 6 feet
   300 × 6 = 1,800 feet deep

7. 100 pounds × 2 = 200 pounds
   100 pounds × 2.8 = 280 pounds
   2.8 times larger

8. How about naming your boat *Filio Mathematica*? (It means "I Love Math" in Latin.)
   14 + 37 + 72 + 22 + 156 + 35 + 24 + 35 + 37 + 95 + 90 + 24 + 129 + 35 + 32 + 20 + 35 + 22 + 72 + 60 + 142 + 46 + 67 + 213 + 26 + 14 + 32 + 72 + 35 + 117 + 37 + 72 + 22 + 67 = 2,008

9.   60 × 3.00 = 180.00
    − 59 × 2.80 = 165.20
    ‾‾‾‾‾‾‾‾‾‾‾‾‾‾‾‾‾‾‾‾
              $14.80

10.   40 × 2.80 = 112.00
    − 39 × 2.60 = 101.40
    ‾‾‾‾‾‾‾‾‾‾‾‾‾‾‾‾‾‾‾‾
              $10.60

11. 20,000 pound quota (see #7) × \$2.80 per pound = \$56,000

12. 11 cents per pound × 1 pound = 11 cents

Air Traffic Controller (pp. 48–50)

1. $\dfrac{120 \text{ miles}}{1 \text{ hour}} = \dfrac{x \text{ miles}}{1 \text{ minute}}$

   $\dfrac{120 \text{ miles}}{60 \text{ minutes}} = \dfrac{x \text{ miles}}{\text{minute}}$

   $\dfrac{2 \text{ miles}}{1 \text{ minute}} = 2 \text{ miles}$

2. Answers will vary. If school is out at 3:00 p.m. = 15:00 (or 1500 hours). If school is out at 3:30 p.m. = 15:30.

3. 1900 minus 1200 is 7 hours. 1900 is later than noon, so the sun must have come up earlier in England.

4. Answers will vary, depending on time zone. Compare your time to Greenwich, England's time, and calculate the difference.

5. $\dfrac{60 \text{ miles}}{60 \text{ minutes}} = \dfrac{1 \text{ mile}}{1 \text{ minute}} = \dfrac{5 \text{ miles}}{5 \text{ minutes}}$
   ETA 0905

6. $\dfrac{120 \text{ miles}}{60 \text{ minutes}} = \dfrac{2 \text{ mile}}{1 \text{ minute}} = \dfrac{10 \text{ miles}}{5 \text{ minutes}}$
   ETA 0905

7. $\dfrac{240 \text{ miles}}{60 \text{ minutes}} = \dfrac{4 \text{ mile}}{1 \text{ minute}} = \dfrac{20 \text{ miles}}{5 \text{ min}}$
   ETA 0905
   All three planes arrive at the same time.

Master Carver (pp. 51–54)

1. The scale is 1 inch to 1 foot (1 inch to 12 inches, or 1 to 12).
   2 ½ feet high × 12 =
   (12 × 2) + (12 × ½) =
   24 + 6 = 30 feet high

2. 4 feet = 12 inches × 4 = 48 inches
   48 inches × 10 = 480 years old
   To determine what year it was when the tree first began to grow, subtract 480 from the year of publication of this book. During the early 1500s, Europeans had discovered this "New World," but Native Americans were the primary inhabitants coast to coast.

3. 1,500 ~~cubic feet~~ × 27 $\dfrac{\text{pounds}}{\text{cubic foot}}$ = 40,500 pounds
   40,500 pounds ÷ 2000 = 20.25 tons

4. 1,500 ~~cubic feet~~ × 23 $\dfrac{\text{pounds}}{\text{cubic foot}}$ = 34,500 pounds
   40,500 − 34,500 = 6,000 pounds (3 tons)

5. It helps to draw a diagram.
   The finished log will be 4 feet − 2 (3 inches + 2 inches) =
   4 feet − 2 (5 inches) =
   48 inches − 10 inches = 38 inches or 3 feet 2 inches

6. There are 52 weeks in a normal year (365 ÷ 7 = 52 weeks + 1 day)
21 days ÷ 7 = 3 weeks
52 weeks + 3 weeks = 55 weeks

7. 3,150 dollars × 30 feet = $94,500
   foot

8. 100 − 15% = 85%
$94,500 × .85 = $80,325

9. 162.5 ÷ 5 = 32.5 times taller

10. 14 ½ × 3 = (14 × 3) + (½ × 3) = 42 + 1 ½ = 43 ½ feet around

11. About 10, but try it!

Diver (pp. 55–58)

1. Yes
⅛ = .125
0.122 is less than 0.125, so the thickness is less than ⅛.

2. 50 feet × 0.5 pound per foot = 25 pounds
25 pounds + 90 pounds = 115 pounds of pressure

3. Yours will look like this:

Ketchikan Tide Levels

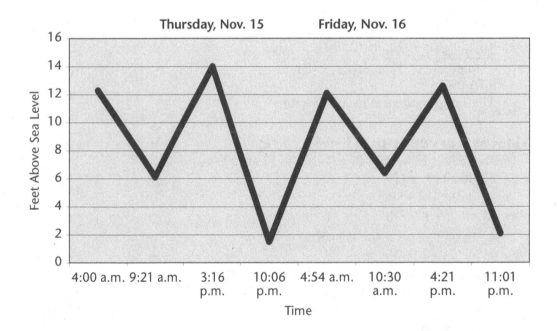

In real life, it's more like this:

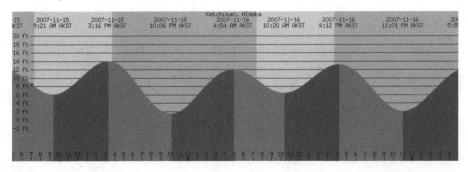

4. 4 dives × 20 minutes per dive = 80 minutes
   $420 per hour ÷ 60 minutes per hour = $7 per minute
   $7 × 80 minutes = $560

5. 90 feet / 30 feet per minute = 3 minutes
   12:01 − 3 minutes = 11:61 − 3 minutes = 11:58 a.m.

Bush Pilot (pp. 59–63)

1. 78 ÷ 17 = 4.58 ≈ 4.6 hours

2. 4.6 = 4 ⁶⁄₁₀ = 4 ³⁶⁄₆₀ = 4 hours and 36 minutes

3. 4 hours 36 minutes
   −   30 minutes
   ‾‾‾‾‾‾‾‾‾‾‾‾‾‾‾‾‾
   4 hours 6 minutes

4. 50 miles round trip @ 120 miles per hour
   We know if she can fly that fast, the answer will be less than 1 hour, so divide the smaller by the larger.
   50 ÷ 120 = 0.4 hours

5. 0.4 hours = ⁴⁄₁₀ = ²⁴⁄₆₀ = 24 minutes

6.   4 hrs 6 min
   −   24 min
   ‾‾‾‾‾‾‾‾‾‾‾‾‾
      3 hrs 66 min
   −   24 min
   ‾‾‾‾‾‾‾‾‾‾‾‾‾
      3 hrs 42 min

7.   120 mph
   − 40 mph
   ‾‾‾‾‾‾‾‾
      80 mph

   $$\frac{25 \text{ miles}}{1} \times \frac{1 \text{ hour}}{80 \text{ miles}} = 0.3 \text{ hours}$$

   $$\frac{0.3 \text{ hours}}{1} \times \frac{60 \text{ minutes}}{1 \text{ hour}} = 18 \text{ minutes}$$

8.   120 mph
   − 60 mph
   ‾‾‾‾‾‾‾‾
      60 mph
      60 mph = 1 mile per minute
      25 miles × 1 minute each = 25 minutes

9.   120
   + 20
   ‾‾‾‾
      140

   $$\frac{25 \text{ miles}}{1} \times \frac{1 \text{ hour}}{140 \text{ miles}} = 0.2 \text{ hours}$$
   0.2 hours × 60 minutes per hour = 12 minutes

10.   78 gallons
      × 6 pounds
      ‾‾‾‾‾‾‾‾‾‾
      468 pounds of fuel
      1060 pounds
   − 468 pounds
      ‾‾‾‾‾‾‾‾‾‾
      592 pounds

73

11. No

       210 pounds
       226 pounds
     + 179 pounds
       615 pounds

12.   1.25 hours
       + 0.50 reserve gas
         1.75 hours
         1.75 hours
       × 17 gallons per hour
        29.75 gallons

13. Yes

        29.75 gallons
      × 6 pounds per gallon
       178.50 pounds of fuel
      1060.0 capacity with Michelle aboard
     − 178.5 pounds of fuel
       881.5 pounds available to carry

About the Author

"My job is to enable students to discover their own brilliance. There's nothing more fun than being out-thought by my own students."

Marya Washington Tyler has taught gifted students for 15 years, and has a master's degree in gifted education. She is the author of several Prufrock bestsellers, including *Real Life Math Mysteries* and *It's Alive!* She cowrote *Extreme Math* with her photographer husband Kip. They have four intrepid, spontaneous, and gifted children of their own.

On-the-Job Math Mysteries evolved from Kip and Marya's experience living in Alaska and now on the Olympic Peninsula, where they kayak, mountain climb, cross-country ski, snowshoe, beach comb and wonder about the infinitely profound and intricate beauty of nature.

Feel free to contact Marya at maryawashingtontyler@hotmail.com.

Common Core State Standards Alignment

Grade Level	Common Core State Standards in Math
Grade 4	4.OA.A Use the four operations with whole numbers to solve problems.
	4.NBT.A Generalize place value understanding for multi-digit whole numbers.
	4.NBT.B Use place value understanding and properties of operations to perform multi-digit arithmetic.
	4.NF.A Extend understanding of fraction equivalence and ordering.
	4.NF.B Build fractions from unit fractions.
	4.NF.C Understand decimal notation for fractions, and compare decimal fractions.
	4.MD.A Solve problems involving measurement and conversion of measurements.
Grade 5	5.NBT.A Understand the place value system.
	5.NBT.B Perform operations with multi-digit whole numbers and with decimals to hundredths.
	5.NF.B Apply and extend previous understandings of multiplication and division.
	5.MD.A Convert like measurement units within a given measurement system.
	5.MD.C Geometric measurement: understand concepts of volume.
Grade 6	6.RP.A Understand ratio concepts and use ratio reasoning to solve problems.
	6.NS.B Compute fluently with multi-digit numbers and find common factors and multiples.
	6.NS.C Apply and extend previous understandings of numbers to the system of rational numbers.
	6.EE.A Apply and extend previous understandings of arithmetic to algebraic expressions.
	6.G.A Solve real-world and mathematical problems involving area, surface area, and volume.
Grade 7	7.RP.A Analyze proportional relationships and use them to solve real-world and mathematical problems.
	7.NS.A Apply and extend previous understandings of operations with fractions.
	7.G.B Solve real-life and mathematical problems involving angle measure, area, surface area, and volume.
Grade 8	8.G.B Understand and apply the Pythagorean Theorem.

Key: OA = Operations & Algebraic Thinking; NBT = Number & Operations in Base Ten; NF = Number & Operations–Fractions; MD = Measurement & Data; G = Geometry; RP = Ratios & Proportional Relationships; NS = The Number System; EE = Expressions and Equations